OFFICIAL SQA PAST PAPERS WITH ANSWERS

INTERMEDIATE 1

ENGLISH
2009-2013

HODDER
GIBSON
LEARN MORE

SQA

Hodder Gibson is grateful to the copyright holders, as credited on the final page of the Question Section, for permission to use their material. Every effort has been made to trace the copyright holders and to obtain their permission for the use of copyright material. Hodder Gibson will be happy to receive information allowing us to rectify any error or omission in future editions.

Hachette UK's policy is to use papers that are natural, renewable and recyclable products and made from wood grown in sustainable forests. The logging and manufacturing processes are expected to conform to the environmental regulations of the country of origin.

Orders: please contact Bookpoint Ltd, 130 Park Drive, Abingdon, Oxon OX14 4SE. Telephone: (44) 01235 827720. Fax: (44) 01235 400454.

Lines are open 9.00–5.00, Monday to Saturday, with a 24-hour message answering service. Visit our website at www.hoddereducation.co.uk. Hodder Gibson can be contacted direct on: Tel: 0141 848 1609; Fax: 0141 889 6315; email: hoddergibson@hodder.co.uk

This collection first published in 2013 by

Hodder Gibson, an imprint of Hodder Education,

An Hachette UK Company

2a Christie Street

Paisley PA1 1NB

{BrightRED   Hodder Gibson is grateful to Bright Red Publishing Ltd for collaborative work in preparation of this book and all
PUBLISHING   SQA Past Paper and National 5 Model Paper titles 2013.

Typeset by PDQ Digital Media Solutions Ltd, Bungay, Suffolk NR35 1BY

Printed in the UK

A catalogue record for this title is available from the British Library

ISBN 978-1-4718-0235-5

3 2 1

2014 2013

Introduction

Study Skills – what you need to know to pass exams!

Pause for thought

Many students might skip quickly through a page like this. After all, we all know how to revise. Do you really though?

Think about this:

"IF YOU ALWAYS DO WHAT YOU ALWAYS DO, YOU WILL ALWAYS GET WHAT YOU HAVE ALWAYS GOT."

Do you like the grades you get? Do you want to do better? If you get full marks in your assessment, then that's great! Change nothing! This section is just to help you get that little bit better than you already are.

There are two main parts to the advice on offer here. The first part highlights fairly obvious things but which are also very important. The second part makes suggestions about revision that you might not have thought about but which WILL help you.

Part 1

DOH! It's so obvious but …

Start revising in good time

Don't leave it until the last minute – this will make you panic.

Make a revision timetable that sets out work time AND play time.

Sleep and eat!

Obvious really, and very helpful. Avoid arguments or stressful things too – even games that wind you up. You need to be fit, awake and focused!

Know your place!

Make sure you know exactly **WHEN and WHERE** your exams are.

Know your enemy!

Make sure you know what to expect in the exam.

How is the paper structured?

How much time is there for each question?

What types of question are involved?

Which topics seem to come up time and time again?

Which topics are your strongest and which are your weakest?

Are all topics compulsory or are there choices?

Learn by DOING!

There is no substitute for past papers and practice papers – they are simply essential! Tackling this collection of papers and answers is exactly the right thing to be doing as your exams approach.

Part 2

People learn in different ways. Some like low light, some bright. Some like early morning, some like evening / night. Some prefer warm, some prefer cold. But everyone uses their BRAIN and the brain works when it is active. Passive learning – sitting gazing at notes – is the most INEFFICIENT way to learn anything. Below you will find tips and ideas for making your revision more effective and maybe even more enjoyable. What follows gets your brain active, and active learning works!

Activity 1 – Stop and review

Step 1

When you have done no more than 5 minutes of revision reading STOP!

Step 2

Write a heading in your own words which sums up the topic you have been revising.

Step 3

Write a summary of what you have revised in no more than two sentences. Don't fool yourself by saying, 'I know it but I cannot put it into words'. That just means you don't know it well enough. If you cannot write your summary, revise that section again, knowing that you must write a summary at the end of it. Many of you will have notebooks full of blue/black ink writing. Many of the pages will not be especially attractive or memorable so try to liven them up a bit with colour as you are reviewing and rewriting. **This is a great memory aid, and memory is the most important thing.**

Activity 2 — Use technology!

Why should everything be written down? Have you thought about 'mental' maps, diagrams, cartoons and colour to help you learn? And rather than write down notes, why not record your revision material?

What about having a text message revision session with friends? Keep in touch with them to find out how and what they are revising and share ideas and questions.

Why not make a video diary where you tell the camera what you are doing, what you think you have learned and what you still have to do? No one has to see or hear it but the process of having to organise your thoughts in a formal way to explain something is a very important learning practice.

Be sure to make use of electronic files. You could begin to summarise your class notes. Your typing might be slow but it will get faster and the typed notes will be easier to read than the scribbles in your class notes. Try to add different fonts and colours to make your work stand out. You can easily Google relevant pictures, cartoons and diagrams which you can copy and paste to make your work more attractive and **MEMORABLE**.

Activity 3 – This is it. Do this and you will know lots!

Step 1

In this task you must be very honest with yourself! Find the SQA syllabus for your subject (www.sqa.org.uk). Look at how it is broken down into main topics called MANDATORY knowledge. That means stuff you MUST know.

Step 2

BEFORE you do ANY revision on this topic, write a list of everything that you already know about the subject. It might be quite a long list but you only need to write it once. It shows you all the information that is already in your long-term memory so you know what parts you do not need to revise!

Step 3

Pick a chapter or section from your book or revision notes. Choose a fairly large section or a whole chapter to get the most out of this activity.

With a buddy, use Skype, Facetime, Twitter or any other communication you have, to play the game "If this is the answer, what is the question?". For example, if you are revising Geography and the answer you provide is "meander", your buddy would have to make up a question like "What is the word that describes a feature of a river where it flows slowly and bends often from side to side?".

Make up 10 "answers" based on the content of the chapter or section you are using. Give this to your buddy to solve while you solve theirs.

Step 4

Construct a wordsearch of at least 10 X 10 squares. You can make it as big as you like but keep it realistic. Work together with a group of friends. Many apps allow you to make wordsearch puzzles online. The words and phrases can go in any direction and phrases can be split. Your puzzle must only contain facts linked to the topic you are revising. Your task is to find 10 bits of information to hide in your puzzle but you must not repeat information that you used in Step 3. DO NOT show where the words are. Fill up empty squares with random letters. Remember to keep a note of where your answers are hidden but do not show your friends. When you have a complete puzzle, exchange it with a friend to solve each other's puzzle.

Step 5

Now make up 10 questions (not "answers" this time) based on the same chapter used in the previous two tasks. Again, you must find NEW information that you have not yet used. Now it's getting hard to find that new information! Again, give your questions to a friend to answer.

Step 6

As you have been doing the puzzles, your brain has been actively searching for new information. Now write a NEW LIST that contains only the new information you have discovered when doing the puzzles. Your new list is the one to look at repeatedly for short bursts over the next few days. Try to remember more and more of it without looking at it. After a few days, you should be able to add words from your second list to your first list as you increase the information in your long-term memory.

FINALLY! Be inspired...

Make a list of different revision ideas and beside each one write **THINGS I HAVE** tried, **THINGS I WILL** try and **THINGS I MIGHT** try. Don't be scared of trying something new.

And remember – "FAIL TO PREPARE AND PREPARE TO FAIL!"

Intermediate 1 English

The course

Intermediate 1 English will give you the opportunity to develop your skills in English, literacy and communication. It is a worthwhile qualification in itself (and can help you to get into college or employment), but it is also excellent preparation for Intermediate 2 English. You will read, discuss, and write about interesting texts throughout the course, and will be given an opportunity to express yourself in your Folio of Writing.

How the course is graded

Your grade in Intermediate 1 English depends on two things:

- your Folio of Writing - this is submitted to the SQA for marking and counts for 20% of your final grade
- the two exam papers you sit in May.

The exams

The Close Reading paper is one hour long and there are 30 marks available. In this paper you have to read a passage of non-fiction writing, and answer questions on it. You will be tested on your skills of understanding, analysis and evaluation.

The Critical Essay paper is 45 minutes long and there are 25 marks available. In this paper you have to write one essay about one of the texts you have studied during your course. You are not allowed to bring texts that you have studied into the exam.

The SQA gives detailed advice in the Candidate Guidance Information section of the Intermediate 1 English page on its website.

Close Reading

Try to read as much as you can. Try to read some non-fiction – articles from newspapers, etc. This is the kind of writing you should expect to see in the Close Reading section of the exam. Most people find the passages interesting and can read and understand them, so don't be too worried about not understanding the Close Reading passage in the exam. It won't be too long either – about 1000 words, at the most. There will be the occasional word that you are not sure about, but you should be able to work out what most words mean from the clues in other words around them.

Try to give yourself the best possible chance by answering all the questions. Most people manage to do this. The questions will take you through the passage in order. Read them carefully and follow the instructions given. Be careful to look in the correct places for your answers: in nearly all questions you will be shown where to look in the passage by line number references. It is a good idea to draw a line across your exam paper at the beginning and the end of the section you have been directed to. (Or you could use a highlighter). You do not need to answer in sentences – bullet points will do.

Watch out for questions which ask you to use your own words. Many people lose marks here, but you will be given credit if you make an effort to use your own words but don't manage to change all the words you are asked to look at. **"In your own words"** will be printed in bold wherever it is needed. Sometimes this type of question will ask you to find a small number of words (called an "expression") from the passage, and then put them into your own words. This is almost like a translation: try to substitute words that mean roughly the same into the expression you have chosen. Don't worry if you think there are words which are impossible to change. It is not always possible to find alternative words. Another type of "own words" question is a kind of summary: you might be asked to find the writer's main points/ideas from a particular section. Here, look at the number of marks available, and try to find the same number of points.

For questions about the techniques used by the writer (analysis questions), aim to give as full an explanation of the technique, and how it adds to the writer's meaning, as you can. Most people can find a simile, or a metaphor, etc, (and are given marks for doing so), but lose marks because they can't explain the effects. They can point to examples of techniques, but are less successful in providing an explanation. Try to practise this.

In questions about the writer's word choice, pick out a word or an expression from the passage and make a comment on the actual word(s) you have chosen. Don't make a general comment about the writer's use of words (eg "the word choice is very negative").

Try to have an awareness of how the writer has put his or her piece of writing together – the structure. If you are asked about how a sentence helps to link ideas, look for words that point forward, or back, and quote them. (You will usually be asked to comment on how something links either forward or back, not both). You might be asked about the ending of the piece. Look for words/ideas from the ending which repeat or sum up earlier ideas.

Critical Essay

Most people sitting the exam find no real difficulty in selecting a question from the Critical Essay paper. The questions are designed to give you the opportunity to show what you have learned about the texts you have studied. You will have to prepare/revise the texts you have studied, but try not to worry about things "not coming up".

The questions often ask you to do two things. Make sure that you do both. One of the common mistakes is to concentrate on just one aspect of the question. This would seriously damage your mark. The most important thing is to try to answer the question. Even though you won't have a lot of time, try to make a quick plan before you write each essay. Once you have decided on a question, try to note down five or six things that you want to say in answer to it. Jot them down on your question paper. This could make up a simple plan for your essay. Make sure you address the key words of the question in the first paragraph of your essay, and go back to these key words throughout.

As you prepare for the exam try to have a clear idea in your head of the themes and ideas of the texts you are planning to write about. If you are clear in your mind about these things, you will be able to answer the questions more successfully. If you don't have a good grasp of the main ideas/themes, and you don't write about them, your essay will end up looking like a list of notes.

Many people worry about learning quotations from the texts they have studied, and think that they have to fit every quotation they have learned into their essays. For drama and poetry, you will certainly be expected to include some quotations, but only ones that would be relevant to the question you are answering. Don't be concerned if you don't get the opportunity to use all of your quotations. When writing about a novel, quotations are much less important. When dealing with a novel or short story it is much more important to write about key episodes, and to describe the main characters and setting, etc.

Keep an eye on the accuracy of your writing in the exam. Remember to divide your writing into paragraphs, and make sure you write in sentences (full stops and capital letters).

The main thing to remember is – answer the question.

Good luck!

Remember that the rewards for passing Intermediate 1 English are well worth it! Your pass will help you get the future you want for yourself. In the exam, be confident in your own ability. If you're not sure how to answer a question trust your own instincts and give it a go anyway – keep calm and don't panic! GOOD LUCK!

INTERMEDIATE 1

2009

[BLANK PAGE]

X115/101

NATIONAL
QUALIFICATIONS
2009

FRIDAY, 15 MAY
1.00 PM – 2.00 PM

ENGLISH
INTERMEDIATE 1
Close Reading

Answer all questions.

30 marks are allocated to this paper.

Read the passage carefully and then answer **all** the questions, **using your own words where asked to do so**.

The questions will ask you to show that:

> you understand **what** the writer has said (main ideas and supporting details) (**Understanding–U**);

> you can identify **how** the writer has said it (techniques of structure and style) (**Analysis–A**);

> you can comment on **how well** the writer has achieved his purpose (using appropriate evidence) (**Evaluation–E**).

A code letter (U, A, E) is used alongside each question to identify its purpose for you.

In this passage, the writer, John Simpson, looks back with surprising affection on an occasion when he was cheated.

ROBBED IN PRAGUE

I have only once in my life been robbed by experts.

It happened in Prague, the capital of the old Czechoslovakia, a few days after what everyone now calls the Velvet Revolution of 1989, when the Communist government was overthrown without a drop of blood being shed. Six years earlier, in 1983, I had made a
5   film there about the way the secret police treated political and religious dissidents, those people who disagreed openly with the government. After that, not surprisingly, I was banned from the country.

When I flew in this time, without a proper visa, I gambled on the fact that the revolution was just starting, and I hoped the government officials I encountered would realise that
10   things were about to change. At Prague airport the man behind the immigration desk looked at me and my passport very long and carefully. Then he examined a message which had come up on his computer. Presumably it told him I was "an enemy of the state". In the end he made up his mind to ignore it. He stamped my passport, and gave me a little wintry smile. I was back.

15   The next few days were wonderful. I had a ringside seat, from which I could watch the end of the whole unpleasant, rotten police state which the Russians had created in Czechoslovakia. Still, it took some time to introduce a new system, and many of the old laws still applied. For instance, changing foreign money into the local currency, called crowns, still had to be done in the long-winded, expensive way of the past. I was short
20   of time, and so I decided to change my money with a tout on the street. That was still illegal, but I decided to take the risk.

I wandered down into the Old Town. Today this is the part that stays open until past midnight, but in those days the streets were quiet by seven-thirty. Most of the shops had closed. It was getting late to find anyone to change money. I walked up and down in my
25   expensive coat, looking exactly like what I was—a Westerner looking for a deal.

It worked. A man came out of an old house and walked beside me. He spoke quietly and looked straight ahead. "You want to change money?" he said in good English.

I said I did.

"How much?"

30   Two hundred dollars, I told him. That was a lot of money in Prague.

"I'm working on the house here," the man whispered. "Come into the hall. It's safer."

I stepped into the hall. It was dark, but the light from the room with the workmen in it was enough for us to see to change money.

"So, two hundred dollars, that's 140,000 crowns," the man said.

35   I showed him my two bills of a hundred dollars each. He looked at them carefully, then handed them back to me and began counting out the Czech notes.

At that instant there was an explosion of rage, and a stocky man came charging down the stairs.

"Oh, no!" shouted the man who was counting out the money. "It's my foreman! He's a
40   real Communist. Quick, give me the dollars. Here's your cash."

He shoved a thick wad of notes into my hand. "Run for it! He'll call the cops!"

I ran for it. What if the authorities caught me? Even now, when Communism was collapsing, I could be in trouble. It would be embarrassing for me, and for the BBC.

45　And yet, even while I was running, something was working away inside my head. How come, if it was so dangerous to be doing a deal with a Westerner, the man had shouted out a warning to me in English? That, surely, would be proof to the foreman that he was up to no good.

I slowed down. No policemen were running through the streets in search of me. I stopped in an alley and pulled the wad of money out of my pocket. There were a couple 50　of one-hundred-crown notes on the top. But the rest seemed less familiar. I had a hollow feeling in my stomach as I looked at them. These notes were all Polish. There was huge inflation in Poland at that time, and the whole thick wad of money I held in my hand was worth about five dollars. If, that is, you could find anyone who would accept them.

55　I had been well and truly robbed.

I turned round and ran back. In the old house the workmen were just packing up, and I spoke to one of them. Yes, there had been a couple of men hanging around. They were probably up to no good, he said. One of the men had gone upstairs, though neither of them was supposed to be there. They weren't working on the house, or 60　anything like that. They just came in off the street. He'd heard one of the men shouting. Had they stolen something from me?

"No, not at all," I said, "nothing like that. No, I'd just been asking the way."

"Oh, asking the way," said the workman with a little grin. "I hope he told you. So why did you come back?"

65　I didn't say anything and walked off. At first I was angry. Two hundred dollars was quite a lot of money to have lost. I felt such an idiot.

As I walked, the spires of the old city shone in the damp evening air. Everything seemed so beautiful. Now this country that I loved so much was free, and I had had the privilege of watching it happen. That was worth vastly more than two hundred dollars.

Adapted from John Simpson, *Twenty Tales from the War Zone*

QUESTIONS

Marks   *Code*

1. (a) Explain **in your own words** why "the *Velvet* Revolution of 1989" (line 3) was unusual.   1   U

   (b) Why does the writer include the expression "those people who disagreed openly with the government" in lines 5–6?   2   A

2. The writer says he "gambled" (line 8) when he flew into Prague "this time".

   Explain **in your own words**

   (a) why he thought he might **not** get into the country on this occasion;   1   U

   (b) why he thought he might get in.   1   U

3. Explain the humour of the sentence "Presumably it told him I was 'an enemy of the state'" (lines 12–13).

   Your answer may focus on **content** or **tone**.   1   A

4. Explain what is surprising about the expression "wintry smile" (line 14).   2   A

5. Comment on the effectiveness of the **metaphor** or **image** "a ringside seat" (line 15).   2   E

6. The writer knew that changing money unofficially was "illegal" (line 21).

   Write down the expression from earlier in the paragraph which introduces the idea of this activity being against the law.   1   U

7. Look at lines 22–25, and then explain in your own words what problem the writer came up against when he tried to change his money.   1   U

8. Explain how one example of the writer's **word choice** in lines 26–36 shows that the Czech man changing the money wanted to be cautious.   2   A

9. Lines 37–41 convey a different mood from the quiet caution shown in lines 26–36.

   (a) Show how an example of the writer's **word choice** effectively conveys this new mood.   2   E

   (b) How does the **punctuation** of the words spoken by the Czech man contribute to this mood?   1   A

   (c) How does any feature of the **sentence structure** of the words spoken by the Czech man match this mood?   1   A

10. The writer tells us "something was working away inside my head" (line 44).

    Using your own words as far as possible, explain fully what was worrying him.   3   U

11. (a) According to lines 49–55, how had the man swindled the writer?   3   U

    (b) How did the writer feel when he realised he had been swindled, and how does he emphasise this?   2   A

12. The workman asks the writer if he has had something stolen from him (line 61).

    What does the workman think of the writer's answer, and how can we tell?   2   U/A

13. From line 67 to the end of the passage, the writer reflects on this experience with pleasure.

    Why is this feeling quite understandable or appropriate?   2   A

                                                     Total   **(30)**

[END OF QUESTION PAPER]

[BLANK PAGE]

[BLANK PAGE]

X115/102

NATIONAL
QUALIFICATIONS
2009

FRIDAY, 15 MAY
2.20 PM – 3.05 PM

ENGLISH
INTERMEDIATE 1
Critical Essay

Answer **one** question only.

Each question is worth 25 marks.

Answer ONE question only, taken from any of the Sections A to E.

In all Sections you may use Scottish texts.

Write the number of the question in the margin of your answer booklet.

The following will be assessed:

- **the relevance of your essay to the question you have chosen**
- **your understanding of the main points of the text(s) through some reference to the relevant areas of content**
- **your explanation of the ways in which aspects of structure/style/language contribute to the meaning/effect/impact of the chosen text(s)**
- **your personal reaction to the content or style of the text(s) supported by some textual reference**
- **the quality and technical accuracy of your writing.**

Each question is worth 25 marks.

SECTION A—DRAMA

Answers to questions in this section should refer to such relevant features as: conflict, character, key scene(s), theme, plot . . .

1. Choose a play which involves conflict between relatives or friends or groups of people.

   Show how the conflict arises and say whether you find the outcome of the conflict satisfactory or not.

2. Choose a play in which a character gains your sympathy because of the way he or she is treated by other characters.

   Describe how the character is treated by the others, and how he or she reacts, and explain why you feel sympathy for the character.

SECTION B—PROSE

Answers to questions in this section should refer to such relevant features as: content, key incident, character, theme, imagery . . .

3. Choose a novel **or** short story which has an important relationship between two people, or between a person and a place.

   Say why the relationship is important and explain what happens to it by the end of the story. Go on to say what you feel about the ending.

4. Choose a novel **or** a short story **or** a piece of non-fiction which deals with a subject which interests you or shocks you.

   Say what the subject is and why it arouses these feelings in you.

SECTION C—POETRY

Answers to questions in this section should refer to such relevant features as: content, word choice, theme, imagery, sound . . .

5. Choose a poem which is mainly about one person's experience.

   Describe the experience and show how the poet uses particular words and phrases to help to make it clear to you how the person feels about the experience.

6. Choose a poem which describes a place or an event.

   Briefly identify the place or event and go on to show how the poet's use of particular words and phrases gives a very clear description of the place or event.

SECTION D—FILM AND TV DRAMA

Answers to questions in this section should refer to such relevant features as: character, use of camera, key sequence(s), editing, sound/music, plot, setting . . .

7. Choose a film **or** TV drama* which uses many special effects.

   Describe some of the special effects and say what they add to your enjoyment of the film or TV drama* as a whole.

8. Choose an important character from a film **or** TV drama* who is involved in a conflict.

   Describe the part he or she plays in the conflict and explain how the conflict is made memorable.

   * "TV drama" includes a single play, a series or a serial.

SECTION E—LANGUAGE

Answers to questions in this section should refer to such relevant features as: vocabulary, accent, dialect, tone, abbreviation, register . . .

9. Consider the language used by groups of people who are all interested in the same sport, or hobby, or job, or who all live in the same place.

   What words and phrases do they use which are special to them, and how do these words and phrases help the members of the group to get along with each other better?

10. Consider the language used in any two advertisements you are familiar with.

    Say which advertisement is more successful in persuading you to buy the product and, by referring to particular examples, explain why you think one is better than the other.

[END OF QUESTION PAPER]

[BLANK PAGE]

INTERMEDIATE 1

2010

[BLANK PAGE]

X115/101

NATIONAL
QUALIFICATIONS
2010

THURSDAY, 13 MAY
9.00 AM – 10.00 AM

ENGLISH
INTERMEDIATE 1
Close Reading

Answer all questions.

30 marks are allocated to this paper.

Read the passage carefully and then answer **all** the questions, **using your own words where asked to do so**.

The questions will ask you to show that:

> you understand **what** the writer has said (main ideas and supporting details) (**Understanding—U**);

> you can identify **how** the writer has said it (techniques of structure and style) (**Analysis—A**);

> you can comment on **how well** the writer has achieved his purpose (using appropriate evidence) (**Evaluation—E**).

A code letter (U, A, E) is used alongside each question to identify its purpose for you.

In this extract from his autobiography, the writer, Bill Bryson, remembers and reflects upon the time he was first taken to Disneyland by his parents.

MONEY WELL SPENT

My father returned home in unusually high spirits, and revealed his startling plans to take us away on a trip over Christmas to some mysterious place.

"You wait. You'll like it. You'll see," was all he would say, to whoever asked. The whole idea of it was unspeakably exciting—we weren't the type of people to do
5 something so rash, so sudden, so unseasonal—but unnerving too, for exactly the same reasons. So on the afternoon of 16 December, when Greenwood, my elementary school, dispatched its happy hordes into the snowy streets to begin three glorious weeks of yuletide relaxation (and school holidays in those days, let me say, were of a proper and generous duration), the family Rambler was waiting out front, steaming extravagantly,
10 even keenly, and ready to cut a trail across the snowy prairies. We headed west as usual, crossed the mighty Missouri River and made our way past Omaha. Then we just kept on going. We drove for what seemed like (in fact was) days across the endless, stubbly snow-blown plains. We passed one enticing diversion after another—Pony Express stations, buffalo licks, a pretty big rock—without so much as a sideways glance from my
15 father. My mother began to look faintly worried.

On the third morning, we caught our first sight of the Rockies—the first time in my life I had seen something on the horizon other than a horizon. And still we kept going, up and through the ragged mountains and out the other side. We emerged in California, into warmth and sunshine, and spent a week experiencing its wonders—its mighty
20 groves of redwoods, the lush Imperial Valley, Big Sur, Los Angeles—and the delicious, odd feel of warm sunlight on your face and bare arms in December: a winter without winter.

I had seldom—what am I saying? I had never—seen my father so generous and care-free. At a lunch counter in San Luis Obispo he invited me—*urged* me—to have a large
25 hot fudge sundae, and when I said, "Dad, are you sure?" he said, "Go on, you only live once"—a sentiment that had never passed his teeth before, certainly not in a commercial setting.

We spent Christmas Day walking on a beach in Santa Monica, and the next day we got in the car and drove south on a snaking freeway through the hazy, warm, endless
30 nowhereness of Los Angeles. At length we parked in an enormous parking lot that was almost comically empty—we were one of half a dozen cars, all from out of state—and strode a few paces to a grand entrance, where we stood with hands in pockets looking up at a fabulous display of wrought iron.

"Well, Billy, do you know where this is?" my father asked, unnecessarily. There wasn't a
35 child in the world that didn't know these fabled gates.

"It's Disneyland," I said.

"It certainly is," he agreed, and he stared appreciatively at the gates as if they were something he had privately commissioned.

For a minute I wondered if this was all we had come for—to admire the gates—and if in
40 a moment we would get back in the car and drive on to somewhere else. But instead he told us to wait where we were, and strode purposefully to a ticket booth where he conducted a brief but remarkably cheerful transaction. It was the only time in my life that I saw two $20 bills leave my father's wallet simultaneously. As he waited at the window, he gave us a broad smile and a little wave.

45 "Am I ill or something?" I asked my mother.

"No, honey," she replied.

"Is Dad ill?"

"No, honey, everybody's fine. Your father's just got the Christmas spirit."

At no point in all my life before or since have I been more astounded, more gratified,
50 more happy than I was for the whole of that day. We had the park practically to
ourselves. We did it all—spun gaily in people-sized teacups, climbed aboard flying
Dumbos, marvelled at the exciting conveniences in the Monsanto All-Plastic House of
the Future in Tomorrowland, enjoyed a submarine ride and riverboat safari, took a
rocket to the moon. (The seats actually trembled. "Whoa!" we all said in delighted
55 alarm.) Disneyland in those days was a considerably less slick and manicured wonder
than it would later become, but it was still the finest thing I had ever seen—possibly the
finest thing that existed in America at the time. My father was positively enchanted with
the place, with its tidiness and wholesomeness and imaginative picture-set charm, and
kept asking why all the world couldn't be like this. "But cheaper, of course," he added,
60 comfortingly returning to character and steering us deftly past a souvenir stand.

The next morning we got in the car and began the thousand-mile trip across desert,
mountain and prairie to Des Moines. It was a long drive, but everyone was very happy.
At Omaha, we didn't stop—didn't even slow down—but just kept on going. And if there
is a better way to conclude a vacation by not stopping in Omaha, then I don't know it.

From Bill Bryson, *The Life and Times of the Thunderbolt Kid* (slightly adapted)

QUESTIONS

Marks Code

1. In the opening paragraph, we read that the writer's father returned "in unusually
high spirits".

   Explain **in your own words** what this tells us about the father's character.   2 U

2. Look at lines 3–6.

   (*a*) The writer tells us that the trip was "unspeakably exciting" (line 4).

   In your own words, give **two** reasons why the family found the prospect of
   the trip "exciting".   2 U

   (*b*) As well as exciting, how else did the family find the prospect of the trip?

   Answer **in your own words**.   1 U

3. Look at lines 7–9.

   Explain how any **one** example of the writer's **word choice** in these lines helps
   emphasise the fact that the writer has pleasant memories of Christmas time when
   he was a boy.   2 A

4. Look at lines 9–10, where the author mentions the family Rambler (a make of
   car).

   What is surprising about the way he refers to it?   1 A

5. What does "endless, stubbly, snow-blown" (lines 12–13) suggest about the plains?   1 A

QUESTIONS (continued)

Marks Code

6. Look at the sentence in lines 13–15.

   (*a*) What is the function of the words in parenthesis (dashes)?   **2 A**

   (*b*) What does the fact that he did not give "so much as a sideways glance" suggest about the writer's father?   **1 U**

7. The writer tells us that when he saw the Rocky Mountains, this was the first time he "had seen something on the horizon other than a horizon" (line 17).

   What does this hint about the appearance of the countryside where he lives?   **1 U**

8. Look at the expression "a winter without winter" (lines 21–22).

   (*a*) What is surprising about this expression?   **1 A**

   (*b*) Show how **other words** in the context make clear what the writer means by "a winter without winter".   **2 U**

9. Show with clear reference to the paragraph in lines 23–27 how the writer puts emphasis on the idea that his father is mean with his money.   **2 A**

10. Show how any **one** example of the writer's **word choice** in lines 30–35 effectively conveys the idea that Disneyland was an impressive place.   **2 E**

11. Look at lines 40–44.

   Explain why it is appropriate for the writer to use the expression "remarkably cheerful" when referring to the "transaction" his father conducts.   **2 A**

12. Look at lines 51–54.

   The writer tells us that his family "did it all".

   How does the **sentence structure** in these lines help convey this idea?   **2 A**

13. What is the effect of the inclusion of "actually" (line 54)?   **1 A**

14. The writer says (line 55) that Disneyland was not as "slick and manicured" then as it was to become.

   What does this expression suggest about Disneyland today?   **2 U**

15. The writer says that his father steered the family "deftly past a souvenir stand" (line 60). Why does this suggest the writer's father was "returning to character"?   **1 U**

16. Consider the passage as a whole. Explain why any **one** aspect of this extract helps to make it an effective piece of autobiographical writing.   **2 E**

Total (30)

[END OF QUESTION PAPER]

X115/102

NATIONAL QUALIFICATIONS 2010	THURSDAY, 13 MAY 10·20 AM – 11·05 AM	**ENGLISH INTERMEDIATE 1** Critical Essay

Answer **one** question only.

Each question is worth 25 marks.

Answer ONE question only, taken from any of the Sections A to E.

In all Sections you may use Scottish texts.

Write the number of the question in the margin of your answer booklet.

The following will be assessed:

- **the relevance of your essay to the question you have chosen**
- **your understanding of the main points of the text(s) through some reference to the relevant areas of content**
- **your explanation of the ways in which aspects of structure/style/language contribute to the meaning/effect/impact of the chosen text(s)**
- **your personal reaction to the content or style of the text(s) supported by some textual reference**
- **the quality and technical accuracy of your writing.**

Each question is worth 25 marks.

SECTION A—DRAMA

Answers to questions in this section should refer to such relevant features as: conflict, character, key scene(s), theme, plot . . .

1. Choose a play in which there is a character who changes during the course of the action.

   Say what the character is like at the beginning of the play, and then go on to explain how he or she changes during the play.

2. Choose a play in which there is a key scene which you found particularly dramatic.

   Say what happens in the scene, and then explain why you think it is important.

SECTION B—PROSE

Answers to questions in this section should refer to such relevant features as: content, key incident, character, theme, imagery, setting . . .

3. Choose a novel **or** a short story which interests you right from the beginning.

   Say what interests you, and explain how the writer keeps you interested in the rest of the story.

4. Choose a novel **or** a short story **or** a piece of non-fiction in which there is a person towards whom you feel a strong emotion such as sympathy **or** hatred **or** admiration.

   Say how you feel about the person, and explain why you feel this way.

SECTION C—POETRY

Answers to questions in this section should refer to such relevant features as: content, word choice, theme, imagery, sound . . .

5. Choose a poem in which a person or a place is described clearly.

   Say who or what is being described, and then go on to show how the poet's use of language makes the description so clear.

6. Choose a poem which has an important message for you.

   Say what the message of the poem is, and then go on to show how the poet uses particular words and phrases to make the poem's message clear.

SECTION D—FILM AND TV DRAMA

Answers to questions in this section should refer to such relevant features as: character, use of camera, key sequence(s), editing, sound/music, plot, setting . . .

7. Choose a film **or** TV drama* which deals with a group of people within a community, workplace, neighbourhood, family . . .

   Say who the key people in the group are, and explain how they maintain your interest in the film or TV drama.

8. Choose a scene or sequence from a film or TV drama* which has a sad **or** an exciting **or** a tense atmosphere.

   Say what happens in the scene or sequence, and explain how the techniques of film or TV drama make this scene sad **or** exciting **or** tense.

* "TV drama" includes a single play, a series or a serial.

SECTION E—LANGUAGE

Answers to questions in this section should refer to such relevant features as: vocabulary, accent, dialect, tone, abbreviation, register . . .

9. Consider the language used by a group of people with a common interest in, for example, an organisation, a sport, a hobby . . .

   Give examples of the special words and phrases used by the group and say why these words and phrases are interesting.

10. Consider the language of advertisements which aim to persuade you to buy something, to support a charity **or** to take better care of your health.

    Consider the language used in your choice of advertisements and say why you think these advertisements are successful.

[END OF QUESTION PAPER]

[BLANK PAGE]

INTERMEDIATE 1

2011

[BLANK PAGE]

X270/101

NATIONAL
QUALIFICATIONS
2011

FRIDAY, 13 MAY
1.00 PM – 2.00 PM

ENGLISH
INTERMEDIATE 1
Close Reading

Answer all questions.

30 marks are allocated to this paper.

Read the passage carefully and then answer **all** the questions, **using your own words where asked to do so**.

The questions will ask you to show that:

you understand **what** the writer has said (main ideas and supporting details) (**Understanding—U**);

you can identify **how** the writer has said it (techniques of structure and style) (**Analysis—A**);

you can comment on **how well** the writer has achieved his purpose (using appropriate evidence) (**Evaluation—E**).

A code letter (U, A, E) is used alongside each question to identify its purpose for you.

IN THE DRIVING SEAT

In this article Lucy McDonald looks into the world of women lorry drivers.

Think of long-distance lorry driving and the images that spring to mind are of burger stands in lay-bys, Yorkie bars and hairy male drivers. But next time you are on the motorway, take a second look at who is behind the wheel of that juggernaut in the slow lane. You may be surprised.

5　Once a rare sight on British roads, women lorry drivers are increasing in number. Better technology has made the driving easier and, along with female-friendly policies from companies, is helping to erode what was once the sole preserve of men.

According to industry experts, demand for qualified drivers currently outstrips supply and there is a deficit of up to 80,000. Although drivers say that the recession means
10　there is less work, attracting more women to the job could solve a potential long-term recruitment problem. And more professional women are finding the prospect of life on the road appealing.

Kaz Horrocks is a long-distance lorry driver. "I was bored in my old job," she says, "and I enjoy the solitude of driving. Every day is different—sometimes I see amazing sunsets
15　and lambs playing in the fields. I love it when you see the year's first hawthorn blossom and know that spring is near."

Neither hawthorn nor lambs are in evidence when I meet Kaz at six o'clock one dismal June morning in a lorry park. About 100 lorries have overnighted here. They are in lines, slumbering giants on the asphalt, their cab curtains drawn tightly as the drivers
20　sleep inside.

As much as 99 per cent of Britain's freight is delivered by road, so next time you are stuck behind a lorry remember that without this workforce there would be no food on the table. This morning Kaz is taking me to deliver frozen meat. Inside her 40-tonne lorry, the cab is almost militarily neat with bunk beds, lots of ingenious storage and a
25　kettle.

We sail around the M25 with a mighty view for miles ahead. "Chelsea tractors" have nothing on us—the windscreen is almost cinematic in its scope. Radio 2 is burbling in the background as we glide along. I am just a tourist, of course—for full-time female truckers the reality of work has its downsides, too. Until recently many truck stops had
30　only male loos, and sleeping overnight in the cab alone would deter many women.

"I've never felt unsafe, though," says Kaz. "There is a certain amount of curiosity from the men about why I'm driving a truck instead of working at a desk but, apart from the occasional snide remark, most of the guys are really friendly."

The lifestyle is solitary by nature, but even more so for women. "There is a male
35　camaraderie that I am excluded from," Kaz says. "It takes a particular kind of woman to drive a truck. It isn't something that a supermodel is going to do—you have to be a tough cookie."

Personally, I enjoy the open road. I feel free when I'm alone in the car, driving far away with nothing for company but my CD collection and talk radio. The journey appeals
40　more than the destination: no bickering children or phone calls, nothing that must be dealt with. And how much more glorious that detachment would feel if you were 6 ft above other road users . . .

The only way to test this happy vision against the other realities that Kaz describes—traffic jams, tight deadlines, aggressive drivers and machismo—is to hit the road myself,
45　although as someone who failed her driving test four times years ago I approach the challenge of HGV training with no little trepidation.

The HGV training normally takes five days, but my instructor has just a morning to show me the rudiments. I climb the ladder into a shiny 17-tonne lorry and feel a shiver as I turn on the ignition. The roar as its engine awakens sends vibrations through my
50 whole body. The lorry is 27 ft (8·2 m) long and 12 ft 6 in (3·8 m) high. My little car would fit quite comfortably in its cabin—possibly twice over. It has 350 horsepower (I am not really sure what this means but it certainly sounds impressive). There are eight gears and no dual control, which does not seem to worry my instructor in the slightest, even when I reveal my chequered driving-test record.

55 I thrust the giant gearstick into first and ease my foot tentatively off the clutch. In principle it is just like in a car, but in practice the difficulty of everything required— effort, concentration, even aim—has been multiplied many times. I start moving and, for the first time in 20 years, remember why I never go on rollercoasters. The excitement is tremendous but so is the fear of something so powerful. I am not only in
60 the grip of a monster but, supposedly, in control of it.

Within 30 minutes I am soaring around the training ground, doing nifty turns and even managing to reverse into a tight parking space. "Despite all the jokes, women are far better drivers than men," my instructor says. "That's why they are cheaper to insure. It's because they can multi-task. I know it's a cliché but it's true. They are better
65 pupils, too—they don't think they know it all as soon as they sit behind the wheel."

The national pass rate for the HGV test is 34 per cent, and although there are no gender-specific statistics available he reckons that the pass rate for women is more like 70 per cent. Improved technology, in particular power steering, has made it easier for women to drive such large vehicles.

70 Yet the driving itself is only one battle in the war to win female hearts and minds—and the easiest. The industry has been male-dominated for so long that life on the road can still be difficult for women, even though equal opportunities legislation has helped.

Adapted from an article by Lucy McDonald in The Times

QUESTIONS

Marks   Code

1. Look at lines 1–7 and then explain **in your own words as far as possible** why we "may be surprised" nowadays when on a motorway.   2 U

2. Look at lines 8–12, and then explain fully **in your own words** what the "recruitment problem" (line 11) is.   2 U

3. Look at lines 13–16, and then explain why what Kaz says helps to make clear why she prefers lorry-driving to her old job.   2 A

4. Explain why the sentence in lines 17–18 works well as a link between paragraphs.   2 A

5. Look at the sentence in lines 21–23, and then explain how any feature of this sentence helps to get across the writer's argument.

   Your answer may concentrate on **content** or on any other feature such as **word choice**, **structure** or **tone**.   2 A/E

6. Comment on the effectiveness of the expression "militarily neat" (line 24) as an **image** or **metaphor**.   2 E

QUESTIONS (continued)

Marks   Code

7. Look at the lines 26–30.

    (*a*) Explain the writer's use of inverted commas round the expression "Chelsea tractors" (line 26).   1   A

    (*b*) Explain the appropriateness of "burbling" in line 27.   1   A

    (*c*) Explain why the writer calls herself "just a tourist" (line 28).   1   U/A

8. In line 31, Kaz Horrocks says that she has "never felt unsafe".

    Explain **in your own words** why this is the case.   2   U

9. We read in line 34 that "The lifestyle is solitary by nature, but even more so for women".

    Explain **in your own words** why this is so.   2   U

10. In line 38, the writer tells us that she feels "free" on the open road.

    Write down the expression from later in the paragraph that sums up her feeling about the experience of driving.   1   U

11. Why does the writer use dashes in lines 43–44?   1   A

12. Look at lines 43–54, and then explain what the writer means when she refers to her "chequered driving-test record" (line 54).   2   U

13. Look at lines 55–60.

    Identify **one** example of **contrast** in the writer's word choice.   2   A

14. Look at lines 61–62, and then show how **one** example of the writer's **word choice** illustrates a point about how her driving improved.   2   A

15. The driving instructor claims that women "are better pupils" (lines 64–65).

    What piece of evidence in the *next* paragraph goes some way towards proving his point?   1   A

16. Think about the passage **as a whole**.

    Explain with reference to the text which of these you think is the main purpose of this article:

    (*a*) to entertain and inform;

    (*b*) to argue or persuade.   2   E

Total (30)

[END OF QUESTION PAPER]

X270/102

NATIONAL
QUALIFICATIONS
2011

FRIDAY, 13 MAY
2·20 PM – 3·05 PM

ENGLISH
INTERMEDIATE 1
Critical Essay

Answer **one** question only.

Each question is worth 25 marks.

Answer ONE question only, taken from any of the Sections A to E.

In all Sections you may use Scottish texts.

Write the number of the question in the margin of your answer booklet.

The following will be assessed:

- **the relevance of your essay to the question you have chosen**
- **your understanding of the main points of the text(s) through some reference to the relevant areas of content**
- **your explanation of the ways in which aspects of structure/style/language contribute to the meaning/effect/impact of the chosen text(s)**
- **your personal reaction to the content or style of the text(s) supported by some textual reference**
- **the quality and technical accuracy of your writing.**

Each question is worth 25 marks.

SECTION A—DRAMA

Answers to questions in this section should refer to such relevant features as: conflict, character, key scene(s), theme, plot . . .

1. Choose a play in which there is conflict between two characters.

   Say what caused the conflict and show how the writer develops it throughout the play.

2. Choose a play in which there is an important incident which acts as a turning point.

   Describe the important incident and show how it affects the rest of the play.

SECTION B—PROSE

Answers to questions in this section should refer to such relevant features as: content, key incident, character, theme, imagery, setting . . .

3. Choose a novel **or** a short story which you enjoyed because of your interest in an important character.

   Say how the writer makes the character interesting for you throughout the novel or short story.

4. Choose a novel **or** a short story **or** a piece of non-fiction which appealed to you because of its theme or topic.

   Say what the theme or topic is and show how the writer makes it appealing.

SECTION C—POETRY

Answers to questions in this section should refer to such relevant features as: content, word choice, theme, imagery, sound . . .

5. Choose a poem which creates a particular feeling in the reader such as fear, sadness, anger, joy . . .

   Say what the feeling is and go on to show how the poet creates this feeling.

6. Choose a poem which describes an important incident.

   Say what the important incident is and show how the poet uses words and phrases to describe it effectively.

SECTION D—FILM AND TV DRAMA

Answers to questions in this section should refer to such relevant features as: character, use of camera, key sequence(s), editing, sound/music, plot, setting . . .

7. Choose a film **or** TV drama* in which a character has to face a problem.

   Describe the problem, and explain how the film **or** programme makers show the character dealing with it.

8. Choose a film **or** TV drama* in which there is an exciting ending.

   Describe briefly the exciting ending, and explain how the film **or** programme makers create the excitement.

   * "TV drama" includes a single play, a series or a serial.

SECTION E—LANGUAGE

Answers to questions in this section should refer to such relevant features as: vocabulary, accent, dialect, tone, abbreviation, register . . .

9. Consider the language used by a particular group of people.

   Give examples of the special words and phrases used by the group, and explain why they are useful and interesting.

10. Consider the language of any advertisement **or** group of advertisements that you have studied.

    Give examples of the language used in your choice of advertisement(s) and say why you think these examples are effective.

[END OF QUESTION PAPER]

[BLANK PAGE]

INTERMEDIATE 1

2012

[BLANK PAGE]

X270/10/01

NATIONAL QUALIFICATIONS 2012	WEDNESDAY, 16 MAY 9.00 AM – 10.00 AM	ENGLISH INTERMEDIATE 1 Close Reading

Answer all questions.

30 marks are allocated to this paper.

Read the passage carefully and then answer **all** the questions, **using your own words where asked to do so**.

The questions will ask you to show that:

> you understand **what** the writer has said (main ideas and supporting details) (**Understanding—U**);

> you can identify **how** the writer has said it (techniques of structure and style) (**Analysis—A**);

> you can comment on **how well** the writer has achieved his/her purpose (using appropriate evidence) (**Evaluation—E**).

A code letter (U, A, E) is used alongside each question to identify its purpose for you.

SKIRL POWER

In this article, the writer tells us that the skirl, or sound, of the pipes is being heard again – and not only in Scotland.

Tucked away close to London Bridge, the Mudlark Pub might normally take a while to find. Tonight, however, you could locate it blindfold. Upstairs, as out of place as a troupe of Oxfordshire morris dancers round the back of Glasgow Central Station, five pipers are playing their hearts out. Even with the windows closed the decibel levels
5 are substantial. They are Manawatu, a Scottish pipe band from New Zealand, whose unison playing is so precise that it sounds like a single instrument. Towards the end they march downstairs into the street where they do a moonlit lap of honour, watched by a slightly bemused-looking crowd.

The Great Highland Bagpipe is an instrument that inspires almost fanatical levels of
10 passion, despite the fact that most players don't even make a living from it. But it is a passion I want to share. And I'm not alone. Piping is on the up. In Scotland, new pipe bands are springing up, and even in London a growing demand has meant that organised classes for adults have started, apparently for the first time since the 1930s. Run by the Scottish Piping Society of London, they cost around £10 for two hours –
15 probably the best-value music tuition in the capital.

Some students have Scottish roots. Others, like me, simply like the idea of a challenge. A competent violinist and pianist and basic recorder player, I've even dabbled in the ukulele. 'So why not tackle the bagpipes?' I think, as I eye a YouTube performance by the Red Hot Chilli Pipers, the closest thing the piping world has to pin-ups. They
20 have teamed the bagpipe with electric guitars and keyboard, punching out dazzling arrangements of rock anthems, attracting new audiences and players in the process.

Adam Sanderson, the vice-president of the society, is swift to reduce my ambitions to more modest levels. "We get lots of calls from men who say, 'I had a Scottish father and I want to learn the bagpipes in two weeks so I can play at my daughter's wedding,'"
25 he says.

But nothing about the bagpipe is easy. The hand position is deceptively like the recorder yet, as Sanderson says, "halfway between and upside down", and the tuning is based on an ancient scale. Most woodwind instruments have a single or double reed. The bagpipe has four. Moisture can flatten the sound; warmth raise it. Simply achieving
30 accurate tuning can be a minor miracle. Then there's the chanter.

With just nine basic notes, pipers use nifty fingerwork that gives the illusion of playing more notes than are actually possible. Modern technology makes life easier. Synthetic reeds keep their pitch for longer. Pipe bags now come with a Gore-Tex lining. And for the "wet" player there are moisture-control systems – boxes filled with absorbent
35 cat litter.

To find out more about what's involved, I go to the Pipe Band World Championships in Glasgow, where judges take just a day to work their way through more than 200 bands from as far away as Australia and Pakistan. It can seem like an inward-facing event. Literally so. As the bands play the marches, reels and strathspeys known as Ceòl Beag,
40 or light music, they turn away from the audience, watching each other so they don't drop a note.

"It gets under your skin," says Alan McGeachie, who plays the pipes and is a drummer with the Strathclyde Police Pipe Band, 12 times winners in the world championships. "It's in your blood. If you decide to leave, you think: 'Thank God I'm away from it', and suddenly it grabs you. It'll be with you to your last day."

45

Which is why, early one morning, I am in a rugby clubhouse in South London to get a preview lesson with Alasdair Smith, one of the instructors of the London piping classes. I've attempted to get to grips with the fingering, using a practice chanter to honking effect. Then I get to try out a full set of pipes – something that, in reality, no beginner would attempt for months. I blow into the bag like a breathalyser. Instead of there being constant pressure to force the air into the drones and chanter, seamlessly topping up the reservoir of air as I go, the bagpipe "sirens" horribly. Only by blocking two of the three drones do I get near a continuous note.

50

Then Smith plays a piece from the bagpipe's classical repertoire, developing into increasingly complex variations. Even to my ears, it's light years away from my enamel-stripping efforts. Piping can become an all-consuming obsession, he says. "I wouldn't want to sell it to anyone. It is enormously difficult and it's a long journey, a striving for perfection. When you're well tuned and well set up, it's uniquely captivating. That's what pipers are striving for." Unfortunately for my neighbours, I'm beginning to have an inkling of what he means.

55

60

Charlotte Phillips, in *The Times*

QUESTIONS
Marks Code

1. The writer tells us that the Mudlark Pub "might normally take a while to find" (lines 1–2).

   Explain **as far as possible in your own words** why this is the case.   1   U

2. Why is it appropriate for the writer to use "however" in line 2?   2   A

3. How effective do you find the comparison "as out of place as a troupe of Oxfordshire morris dancers round the back of Glasgow Central Station" (lines 2–3)?   2   E

4. Explain **in your own words** what is meant by "the decibel levels are substantial" (lines 4–5).   2   U

5. Why does the writer find it surprising that "The Great Highland Bagpipe is an instrument that inspires almost fanatical levels of passion" (lines 9–10)?

   Explain as far as possible **in your own words**.   1   U

6. Explain **in your own words two** pieces of evidence the writer gives to support her claim that "Piping is on the up" (line 11).   2   U/A

7. **Using your own words as far as possible**, give **two** reasons why the writer thought she might "tackle the bagpipes" (line 18).   2   U

QUESTIONS

Marks *Code*

8. What does the writer suggest about the group the Red Hot Chilli Pipers by comparing them to "pin-ups" (line 19)?

1   U

9. Explain why any example of the writer's **word choice** in the sentence in lines 19–21 effectively conveys how impressive the band are.

2   A

10. The writer says "reduce my ambitions to more modest levels" (lines 22–23).

Explain **in your own words** what this means.

2   U

11. Explain why the sentence "But nothing about the bagpipe is easy" (line 26) works well at this point in the passage.

2   A

12. Explain why the writer uses inverted commas round "wet" (line 34).

1   A

13. Why does the writer include the expression "or light music" (line 40)?

1   U/A

14 The player Alan McGeachie says that pipe music "gets under your skin" and is "in your blood" (lines 42–44).

Explain how **one** expression later in the paragraph shows what he means.

2   A

15. Look at lines 48–52.

Explain how any expression from these lines shows that the writer is not impressed by the **sounds** she makes.

2   A

16. Explain how effective you find any part of the expression "light years away from my enamel-stripping efforts" (lines 55–56) in illustrating the difference between Alasdair Smith's playing and the writer's.

2   E

17. Explain why it is unfortunate for her neighbours that the writer is beginning to see what Smith means (see lines 59–60).

1   U

18. Think about the passage as a whole.

Why might "Skirl Power" be considered an appropriate title for this article?

2   E

Total (30)

[END OF QUESTION PAPER]

X270/10/02

NATIONAL
QUALIFICATIONS
2012

WEDNESDAY, 16 MAY
10.20 AM – 11.05 AM

ENGLISH
INTERMEDIATE 1
Critical Essay

Answer **one** question only.

Each question is worth 25 marks.

Answer ONE question only, taken from any of the Sections A to E.

In all Sections you may use Scottish texts.

Write the number of the question in the margin of your answer booklet.

The following will be assessed:

- **the relevance of your essay to the question you have chosen**
- **your understanding of the main points of the text(s) through some reference to the relevant areas of content**
- **your explanation of the ways in which aspects of structure/style/language contribute to the meaning/effect/impact of the chosen text(s)**
- **your personal reaction to the content or style of the text(s) supported by some textual reference**
- **the quality and technical accuracy of your writing.**

Each question is worth 25 marks.

SECTION A—DRAMA

Answers to questions in this section should refer to such relevant features as: conflict, character, key scene(s), theme, plot . . .

1. Choose a play which has an important concern (such as teenage issues, poverty, family matters . . .).

   Say what the concern is and go on to show how successfully **or** unsuccessfully it is dealt with by at least one of the characters.

2. Choose a play which has a scene which you would regard as important.

   Say what happens in this scene and explain why you think it is important in the play as a whole.

SECTION B—PROSE

Answers to questions in this section should refer to such relevant features as: content, key incident, character, theme, imagery, setting, description, ideas . . .

3. Choose a novel **or** a short story **or** a piece of non-fiction **or** a group of texts which deals with a subject that you found amusing **or** sad **or** that made you angry.

   Say what the subject is and why it aroused these feelings in you.

4. Choose a novel **or** a short story which has a frightening **or** a surprising incident.

   Describe the incident and show how the author's description of the incident and the characters involved makes it frightening or surprising.

SECTION C—POETRY

Answers to questions in this section should refer to such relevant features as: content, word choice, theme, imagery, sound . . .

5. Choose a poem which describes an important incident **or** event.

   Say what the important incident **or** event is and show how the poet uses words and phrases to describe it clearly.

6. Choose a poem which has an important message for you.

   Say what the message of the poem is, and then go on to show how the poet makes the message clear.

SECTION D—FILM AND TV DRAMA

Answers to questions in this section should refer to such relevant features as: character, use of camera, key sequence(s), editing, sound/music, plot, setting . . .

7. Choose a film **or** TV drama* that is concerned with present-day problems.

   Say what the problems are and show how they are presented in an interesting way.

8. Choose a key scene **or** sequence from a film **or** TV drama* which creates a turning point.

   Describe what happens in the scene **or** sequence, and explain why this scene is important to the film **or** TV drama as a whole.

   * "TV drama" includes a single play, a series or a serial.

SECTION E—LANGUAGE

Answers to questions in this section should refer to such relevant features as: vocabulary, accent, dialect, tone, abbreviation, register . . .

9. Consider the language of advertising aimed at a specific age group of people.

   Explain some of the language features used and show how these features would appeal to your chosen age group.

10. Consider any aspect of language use which you have studied and enjoyed.

    Explain which aspect of language use you most enjoyed studying in your investigation and go on to explain why you would encourage other people your age to carry out a similar investigation.

[END OF QUESTION PAPER]

[BLANK PAGE]

INTERMEDIATE 1

2013

[BLANK PAGE]

X270/10/01

NATIONAL
QUALIFICATIONS
2013

FRIDAY, 17 MAY
9.00 AM – 10.00 AM

ENGLISH
INTERMEDIATE 1
Close Reading

Answer all questions.

30 marks are allocated to this paper.

Read the passage carefully and then answer **all** the questions, **using your own words where asked to do so**.

The questions will ask you to show that:

> you understand **what** the writer has said (main ideas and supporting details) (**Understanding—U**);

> you can identify **how** the writer has said it (techniques of structure and style) (**Analysis—A**);

> you can comment on **how well** the writer has achieved his/her purpose (using appropriate evidence) (**Evaluation—E**).

A code letter (U, A, E) is used alongside each question to identify its purpose for you.

PLEASE DON'T KILL OFF OUR NURSERY RHYMES

Studies suggest that learning nursery rhymes builds children's confidence and can help with reading skills.

Coming home from nursery, my daughter Ava, 3, recites *Humpty Dumpty*. "Daddy," she says. "Did you know, Humpty Dumpty is an egg?" She ponders for a moment, her brow furrowed: "But Daddy, eggs don't have legs! And eggs don't have bums. So how can he sit on a wall?" This leads to a lengthy discussion about other things eggs don't
5   possess—such as eyebrows, nostrils and bicycles.

Nursery rhymes have always been part of Ava's life. But a recent survey has shown that nursery rhymes are falling out of favour, with parents claiming they are too old-fashioned to interest children. According to the survey, only 36 per cent of parents in the UK regularly use nursery rhymes, while almost a quarter admit they have never
10 sung one with their child.

It's sad that so many parents don't even think about nursery rhymes. Our goal is to encourage children to have a love of books but, before that, it's about living in a language-rich environment—and rhymes are part of that. They're also tremendously valuable as a confidence-builder. What you find out about yourself when you learn a
15 rhyme and then get a round of applause is really important.

More than 20 per cent of young parents claimed not to use rhymes because they don't consider them "educational". Yet numerous studies report a significant relationship between nursery rhyme knowledge at the age of 3 and success in reading and spelling at 5 and 6. The reasons are complex, but the theory is this: the better children are at
20 detecting syllables and rhymes at an early age, the quicker and more successful their progress with reading. Familiarity with nursery rhymes appears to help. They have an educational value we still don't entirely understand. They enable children to become interested in the rhythm and patterns of language in a way that listening to stories doesn't provide.

25 I arranged to sit in on the "music" sessions at Ava's nursery to see what role nursery rhymes have in the education of preschool children, and if children have the foggiest idea what they mean.

The singalongs usually consist of half traditional nursery rhymes and half original compositions, where the appeal lies in repetitive melody and strong rhythmic element.
30 Rhymes with actions, such as *Incey Wincey Spider*, are especially good for early learning. Some kids can't sit still for long, so these rhymes help them to focus.

The group start with *Ring a Ring o' Roses*, with its much-loved cue to "all fall down". The children love it. Next, *The Grand Old Duke of York*. Afterwards, the class discusses the words. The teacher asks, "Where does the Grand Old Duke march up to?" Blank
35 expressions. It's clear that they just sing along with the sounds.

Next, it's *Baa Baa Black Sheep*. Out of 12 children, ten claim that this is their favourite. Ask them what it's about and once again they haven't a clue. "Who does the sheep give some wool to?" asks the teacher. Silence. She gives them a hint: "He gives some to the master, and some to . . .

40 "The Dane!" exclaims one two-year-old.

At this point a little girl breaks into a rendition of "I'm a Barbie girl, in a Barbie world." Which neatly brings us on to adverts. If we're looking to point a finger of blame for the death of nursery rhymes, we could look at toys and clothes companies with jingles that worm into our brains.

45 The Simpsons portrayed this in an episode where the family celebrates Maggie's first birthday. "Let's all sing a song," suggests Marge. There are blank looks, then the family circuits the dining table, flapping their arms and singing "I feel like chicken tonight". TV theme tunes are nearly as bad. I ask one little girl in the group what her favourite nursery rhyme is and she replies: "Postman Pat."

50 The session is drawing to a close and the teacher opens a bag of teddy bears and passes them round. "We're going to sing *Rock-a-Bye Baby* to help our teddies get to sleep." Millie, 3, suddenly pipes up. "I don't like *Rock-a-Bye Baby*," she says firmly.

Why not? "Because the baby falls."

The others have never considered these lines, said to originate from Native American
55 mothers placing their babies in hammocks suspended from the low branches of a tree.

The nursery manager rejects the idea that nursery rhymes are not educational: "The more obscure ones are almost better because they open up the children's imagination. It doesn't matter if they understand the meaning or not—rhymes introduce them to new words and give them different ideas."

60 It's certainly true that, while most of the entertainment to which children are exposed reflects things which are familiar to them, nursery rhymes conjure up a world that is out of time. Some argue that rhymes stimulate the imagination in unwanted ways. There's no question that they often contain unsettling imagery. *Oranges and Lemons*, for example, ends with the lines "Here comes a candle to light you to bed/Here comes a
65 chopper to chop off your head".

I still remember being shocked, as a child, by the farmer's wife in *Three Blind Mice* chopping off their tails with a carving knife. Indeed, whipping, chopping and beating are all part of your average rhyme. Yet there is no evidence of children being upset by the brutal imagery in nursery rhymes. It is possible that this is because it is "distanced"
70 through the experience of play, like the violence of cartoons like *Tom and Jerry* seems to be.

Nursery rhymes are a free resource—something that involves language and action and a handover of learning. They're a springboard into the world of books, because if children know rhymes, they can open a book, see them there and match their memory
75 to what they see on the page. Educationally they're a wonderfully flexible tool. It would be a tragedy if they disappeared.

Damon Syson, in *The Times*

QUESTIONS   *Marks   Code*

1. What does "her brow furrowed" (lines 2–3) suggest about the writer's little girl?   1   U

2. (a) Look at lines 6–10 and then explain **in your own words** what has happened because parents think nursery rhymes are "too old-fashioned to interest children".   1   U

    (b) How does the writer try to prove this point?   1   A

3. Look at lines 11–15, and then explain **in your own words two** reasons why "It's sad that so many parents don't even think about nursery rhymes".   2   U

QUESTIONS (continued)

Marks Code

4. Explain **fully** why it is appropriate for the writer to use "Yet" (line 17) at this point in his argument.

3   U/A

5. Explain why the writer uses a colon (:) in line 19.

2   A

6. Look at lines 25–27, and then explain why this paragraph works well as a link between sections of the writer's account.

2   A

7. Look at lines 28–39.

   (*a*) Explain **in your own word**s why *Incey Wincey Spider* is "especially good for early learning".

   2   U

   (*b*) What do the children's responses to the teacher's questions about the words of rhymes confirm?

   1   U

   (*c*) What is noticeable about the **structure** of the sentences in which these responses are indicated?

   1   A

8. How effective do you find the writer's use of the sentence which begins "At this point" (line 41)?

2   E

9. How effective do you find the expression "jingles that worm into our brains" (lines 43–44) as an **image** or **metaphor**?

2   E

10. Show how **one** example of the **word choice** in lines 50–53 suggests something about the little girl's character.

2   A

11. The writer acknowledges that "rhymes stimulate the imagination in unwanted ways" (line 62), and goes on to illustrate what he means by this.

   Explain **in your own words** what his point is.

2   U

12. (*a*) Explain why the writer uses inverted commas round "distanced" in line 69.

   1   A

   (*b*) How does the reference to *Tom and Jerry* cartoons help the writer's argument here?

   2   A

13. Think about the passage **as a whole**.

   (*a*) Explain how effective you find any part of the final paragraph as a conclusion to the passage.

   2   E

   (*b*) Explain briefly to what extent the writer has persuaded you that "It would be a tragedy" (lines 75–76) if nursery rhymes disappeared.

   1   E

Total (30)

[END OF QUESTION PAPER]

[BLANK PAGE]

X270/10/02

| NATIONAL QUALIFICATIONS 2013 | FRIDAY, 17 MAY 10.20 AM – 11.05 AM | ENGLISH INTERMEDIATE 1 Critical Essay |

Answer **one** question only.

Each question is worth 25 marks.

Answer ONE question only, taken from any of the Sections A to E.

In all Sections you may use Scottish texts.

Write the number of the question in the margin of your answer booklet.

The following will be assessed:

- **the relevance of your essay to the question you have chosen**

- **your understanding of the main points of the text(s) through some reference to the relevant areas of content**

- **your explanation of the ways in which aspects of structure/style/language contribute to the meaning/effect/impact of the chosen text(s)**

- **your personal reaction to the content or style of the text(s) supported by some textual reference**

- **the quality and technical accuracy of your writing.**

Each question is worth 25 marks.

SECTION A—DRAMA

Answers to questions in this section should refer to such relevant features as: conflict, character, key scene(s), theme, plot . . .

1. Choose a play in which two or more characters have conflicting views on at least one matter of importance.

    Say what these views are and go on to explain how the conflict is developed in the play.

2. Choose a play which catches your interest because of the characters and the events it contains.

    Explain why you find the characters and the events of the play interesting.

SECTION B—PROSE

Answers to questions in this section should refer to such relevant features as: content, key incident, character, theme, imagery . . .

3. Choose a novel **or** a short story **or** a piece of non-fiction in which there is a character **or** a person with whom you feel sympathy.

    Say why you feel sympathy for the character and show how the writer makes you feel this way.

4. Choose a novel **or** a short story **or** a piece of non-fiction which has a shocking **or** unexpected ending.

    Briefly say what happens in the story and then go on to show how the author makes the ending shocking or unexpected.

SECTION C—POETRY

Answers to questions in this section should refer to such relevant features as: content, word choice, theme, imagery, sound . . .

5. Choose a poem which creates an atmosphere which is happy **or** sad **or** frightening **or** dramatic.

   Say what the atmosphere is and go on to show how the poet creates this feeling.

6. Choose a poem in which a person **or** an animal **or** a place is described clearly.

   Say who **or** what **or** where is being described, and then go on to show how the poet's use of language makes the description clear.

SECTION D—FILM AND TV DRAMA

Answers to questions in this section should refer to such relevant features as: character, use of camera, key sequence(s), editing, sound/music, plot, setting . . .

7. Choose a film **or** TV drama* in which there is conflict between two people **or** two groups of people.

   Say what the conflict is about and show how it develops throughout the film **or** TV drama.

8. Choose a film or TV drama* which is mainly about characters facing a difficulty.

   Briefly say what the whole film **or** TV drama is about and show how the film **or** TV drama keeps you interested in the characters.

   * "TV drama" includes a single play, a series or a serial.

SECTION E—LANGUAGE

Answers to questions in this section should refer to such relevant features as: vocabulary, accent, dialect, tone, abbreviation, register . . .

9. Consider the language of advertising in newspapers and magazines **or** on television **or** on radio **or** through the internet.

   Choose **one** advertisement and say how it is successful in persuading you to buy the product.

10. Consider the language used by two different age groups, for example teenagers and older people.

    Give some examples of the vocabulary **and/or** language construction used by each group and explain the reasons for these differences.

[END OF QUESTION PAPER]

Acknowledgements

Permission has been sought from all relevant copyright holders and Hodder Gibson is grateful for the use of the following:

An extract adapted from 'Twenty Tales from the War Zone' by John Simpson, published by Pan MacMillan, London. Reproduced by permission of Pan MacMillan (2009 Close Reading pages 2 & 3).

An extract from 'The Life and Times of the Thunderbolt Kid' by Bill Bryson. Published by Black Swan. Reprinted by permission of The Random House Ltd (2010 Close Reading pages 2 & 3);

An extract from the article 'In The Driving Seat' by Lucy McDonald taken from 'The Times' © The Times/NI Syndication 11 June 2009 (2011 Close Reading pages 2 & 3);

The article 'Skirl Power' by Charlotte Phillips © The Times/NI Syndication 29 Aug 2008 (2012 Close Reading pages 2 & 3);

The article 'Please don't kill off our nursery rhymes' by Damon Syson © The Times/NI Syndication 8 December 2009 (2013 Close Reading pages 2 & 3).

INTERMEDIATE 1 | ANSWER SECTION

ENGLISH INTERMEDIATE 1 CLOSE READING 2009

1. (a) There was no violence/injury

   (b) It explains/clarifies/tells us what "dissidents" means

2. (a) He was proscribed/barred/prohibited/excluded (gloss of "banned")

   or

   Because he did not have the right/correct/required travel document/permission

   (b) There was an alteration of/development in the political circumstances/There was an expectation of leniency

3. Content – (obvious) exaggeration/hyperbole/ overstatement
   Tone – (idea of being) laconic/self-deprecating/ ironic/sardonic
   or mock-seriousness of "enemy of the state"

4. "Wintry" suggests unfriendliness/cold whereas "smile" suggests friendliness/warmth

5. Derivation/sense of 'ringside seat' +
   relationship/appropriateness to writer's situation
   Eg Just as a ringside seat is close to the action/affords a good view (at eg a circus or boxing match)
   So he was very near to/witnessed clearly the (spectacular) end of Communism/the changes in the country.

6. '(a) tout (on the street)'

7. There were (very) few people around (gloss of "the streets were quiet").

8. Quotation of and comment on any of:

walked beside me	(eg) suggests concealment of ongoing transaction
He spoke quietly	(eg) does not wish to draw attention to himself
(he) looked straight ahead	(eg) does not wish to appear shifty/does not want to be seen talking to Simpson
the man whispered	(eg) does not wish to draw attention to himself
(Come into the hall.) It's safer.	(eg) shows concern about/awareness of danger
He looked at them carefully	(eg) shows wariness/prudence

9. (a) Any one of "explosion", "rage", "charging", "Oh, no!", "shouted", "Quick", "shoved", "Run for it" or "call the cops" (clearly) suggests tension/anxiety/ urgency **or** noise

   (b) Use of (several) exclamation marks

   (c) Very brief **or** (idea of) imperative **or** (cumulative effect of) list (of urgent instructions)

10. Some attempt at glosses of:

Although it was "dangerous to be doing a deal with a Westerner"	eg it was risky to do business with someone from the west
"the man had shouted out a warning … in English"	eg the alarm had been called in English
Which was certain "proof … that he was up to no good"	eg which is confirmation he was doing something wrong/illegal

11. (a) Underneath the Czech money on top
    There was Polish money
    Which was worth much less than/worth $2\frac{1}{2}$ % of his money
    And/or very hard to change

    (b) He felt empty/shocked
    He uses "hollow feeling" **or** "well and truly";
    or
    He describes himself as having been "robbed";
    or
    He gives the sentence a paragraph to itself.
    or gloss of "angry" (eg. cross) and reference to "At first I was angry" **or** foolish/embarrassed/and reference to "I felt such an idiot"

12. Incredulity/he does not believe him
    Shown by any one of:
    He grins/he says "I hope he told you"/the repetition of "asking the way"/he asks him why he came back/ appropriate comment on the tone he uses.

13. He had been swindled <u>by experts</u>
    and he was happy to have paid for the experience/he has learned something
    or
    The (incipient) freedom of the country (which he loved) was (considerably) more valuable than his money

ENGLISH INTERMEDIATE 1 CRITICAL ESSAY 2009

Please see critical Essay Marking Principles on pages 69–70.

ENGLISH INTERMEDIATE 1
CLOSE READING
2010

1. Glosses of "unusually" and "high spirits"
   eg he was normally less cheerful
   Or he was more cheerful than usual

2. (a) *Any two from:*
   Reference to "we weren't the type of people" –
   eg this was out of character
   OR reference to "all he would say" – eg idea of
   mystery/suspense/lack of information
   OR gloss of "rash" – eg impulsive/ill-advised/
   impetuous/reckless
   OR gloss of "sudden" – eg unexpected/happening at very
   short notice
   OR gloss of "unseasonal" – eg at an unusual time of year

   (b) Gloss of "unnerving" – eg frightening/scary/
   unsettling/daunting/it made them nervous/uneasy

3. Quotation of and comment on any one of:

happy hordes	eg gives idea of enjoyment (for many) OR is alliterative
snowy streets	eg (stereotypical) attractive scene OR is alliterative
(three) glorious (weeks)	eg gives idea of intensity of pleasure
yuletide	eg suggests nostalgia (because it is old-fashioned)
relaxation	eg suggests (pleasurable) leisure, repose
school holidays (in those days) were … proper/generous	eg conveys sense of approval

4. Makes it sound as if it was human/was alive/had emotions;
   personifies it
   OR reference to "steaming" + extrapolation – eg it is an
   unusual word to use to refer to a car/it is an internal
   combustion engine/or there is a lengthy journey imminent and
   it sounds as if it is malfunctioning

5. They go on for ever/were repetitive/boring/ unattractive/bleak

6. (a) They exemplify/illustrate what is meant by an "enticing
   diversion"
   OR
   They provide humour
   By irony/the examples not being enticing

   (b) He was determined to carry on OR he was not distracted
   by/interested in the things they passed/scenery

7. It is very flat/there are no hills/it is featureless

8. (a) It appears to contradict itself/idea of paradox

   (b) "warm sunlight" or "bare arms"
   suggests unseasonal weather/is unusual for December

9. *Any one expression plus comment – answer may be concerned
   with a feature of word choice, structure, typography or content*

   Word choice

writes "what am I saying?"	which suggests/conveys inadequacy of "seldom"
uses "never"	which suggests lack of precedent
uses "urged"	which suggests shock at the unusual/unexpected generosity
"certainly not"	underlines the rarity of this

   Structure

(Parallelism/ similarity of) "I had seldom … I had never"	draws attention to the contrast/rarity
repetition of "never"	confirms/underlines lack of precedent
use of parenthesis	draws attention to the writer's surprise (at his father's behaviour)
pairing of "seldom … never" or "invited … urged"	is use of/progression to a stronger word

   Typography

italics on "urged"	suggest writer is surprised

   Content

asks his father if he is sure	which suggests surprise
idea that this "sentiment … had never passed his teeth before"	confirms unprecedented nature of this invitation
Another example of the father's behaviour	+ explanation of how this highlights his meanness

10. *Any one example plus comment from:*

enormous parking lot	(clearly) suggests large-scale operation
a grand entrance	(clearly) suggests size/magnificence
fabulous display	(clearly) suggests it was remarkable/extraordinary
fabled gates	(clearly) suggests fame or near-magical quality

11. His father is in good spirits
    Yet he is spending (an unprecedented sum of) money
    The **unexpected** nature of his demeanour must be present
    for full marks.

12. List format
    suggests multiplicity of activities
    OR
    Variety/number of verbs (accept "words") used
    suggests diversity of activities
    OR
    Dash implies expansion
    of "all"

13. To show the boy's wonder/to show the realistic effect (Then);
OR
to convey irony/idea of (retrospective) whimsy at the
unspectacular device (Now)

14. It is (more) efficient/(better or) well-organised; accept also
reference to the pejorative sense of insincerity/ superficiality
(Result)
it is very neat/has been given a face-lift/make-over/has been
done up (Process)

15. He was (adroit/skilful/smart/nifty/nimble at) avoiding
spending money

16. The way the extract
  - uses the first person narration/is written from the writer's
    point of view
  - uses mainly sequential narrative
  - reveals the writer's personality
  - recreates characters/places that have influenced the writer
  - provides details of the writer's history
  - establishes setting in place/time
  - recreates key experiences from the writer's life
  - establishes rapport with the reader
  plus comment on appropriateness to autobiographical writing

ENGLISH INTERMEDIATE 1
CRITICAL ESSAY
2010

Please see critical Essay Marking Principles on pages 69–70.

ENGLISH INTERMEDIATE 1
CLOSE READING
2011

1. an HGV / freight / wagon / truck driver
could well be female / a lady

2. shortfall in / insufficiency of / lack of (gloss of "demand
outstrips supply" or "deficit")
experienced / trained / certified drivers (gloss of "qualified")

3. She likes being on her own OR the variety of (what she sees
when she is) driving (lift or gloss of "solitude" or "Every day
is different")
which is the opposite of the tedium / sameness / monotony of
what she used to do (lift or gloss of "bored")

4. "hawthorn" or "lambs"
refers back to the previous paragraph

5. **Content**

Reference to 99% of freight being road-borne OR reference to (potential absence of) food	(effectively) shows how dominant / important road haulage is
Reference to being stuck behind a lorry	(effectively) shows writer's awareness that lorries can be irksome / acknowledges reality

Word choice

(idea of) imperative "remember"	(effectively) is forceful / personal
or "workforce"	suggests (e.g.) unity of drivers
or reference to the alliteration	emphasises / draws attention to the expression

Structure

Positioning of opening clause	(effectively) underlines the Importance of the statistic
or length of sentence	complements the idea of a long queue

Tone

The forceful / severe / admonitory tone	(effectively) underlines the importance of lorry drivers

Register

Use of second person "you" / direct addressing of the reader	(effectively) involves the reader / shows relevance of the argument to the reader

Typography

Use of figures	(effectively / dramatically) clarifies argument

6. Just as army routine is well-ordered / disciplined / efficient
so the cab is orderly / well-organised / tidy / systematic /
efficiently laid out
or
The bunk beds
are redolent of a barrack-room

7. (a) To acknowledge slang term / (idea of) neologism /
quotation of what other people call the vehicle / The car is
not really a tractor

(b) Meaning: conveys sense of rambling / vacuity / continuity /
lack of attention being paid to it / being at a low volume
Sound: (idea of) onomatopoeia / alliteration

(c) she is only visiting this lifestyle temporarily / for a limited
period /

she is not full time (time)
superficially (depth)
She only sees the good things about the job
She is just a passenger, not the driver

8. (The majority of) her (male) colleagues are affable / nice / just interested
(gloss of "curiosity" or "(most of) the guys are really friendly")
or
There is only the odd mean / nasty / unpleasant / cutting / hurtful comment
(gloss of "the occasional snide remark")
or
She is resilient / hard (gloss of "tough cookie")
And therefore unlikely to be scared

9. She is barred from / prohibited from / not allowed in to / kept out of (gloss of excluded)
(masculine) bonding / comradeship / society / fellowship (gloss of cameraderie)

10. Detachment

11. The words are in parenthesis / they explain / exemplify (what the "realities" are) / indicate the addition of extra information

12. She was unsuccessful in her test
many times / more than once
Some attempt to gloss "someone who failed her driving test four times years ago"

13. (1) "thrust" and "ease" or "tentatively""
(2) "in principle" and "in practice"
(3) "excitement" and "fear"
(4) "in the grip" and "in control"

14.
Within 30 minutes	suggests speed of learning
soaring	suggests (e.g.) confidence
nifty	suggests (e.g.) adroitness
even	indicates particular difficulty of mastered manoeuvre
managing	suggests (new) accomplishment / ability
reverse into a tight parking space	indicates nature of mastered manoeuvre

15. Superior pass rate.

16. No marks for choice. Credit is given for a full answer which gives a valid substantiated point to support the choice, e.g.:

To entertain and inform
uses informal register to connect with reader + example
use of humour / stereotypes + example
use of dramatic description + example
provides many facts + example
quotes / uses appropriate figures / statistics + example
cites evidence from experts + example

To argue or persuade
obvious stance / commitment / conviction + example
use of supporting figures / statistics + example
use of expert witnesses + example
quotes direct testimony / opinions of lady driver + example
uses emotive language + example
forceful tone appropriate to argument + example

ENGLISH INTERMEDIATE 1
CRITICAL ESSAY
2011

Please see critical Essay Marking Principles on pages 69–70.

ENGLISH INTERMEDIATE 1
CLOSE READING
2012

1. Gloss of "tucked away" – eg hidden/not easily seen/inconspicuous/unobtrusive/discreet/out of the way
or
Idea of being overshadowed/dominated by London Bridge

2. There is a contrast between what is usual and what is happening on this occasion eg, "tonight is an exception"
or
Something different is happening on this occasion
Lifts are acceptable, for example:
"Because you could find it blindfold/easily on this occasion/tonight but/though it's usually hard to find"

3.
Effective	It suggests the unexpectedness/strangeness/incongruity/a difference of cultures of bagpipers and/or morris dancers in these settings E.g. "You wouldn't expect to see morris dancers in Glasgow **or** you wouldn't expect to see bagpipers in London"	
Ineffective	The idea that the image doesn't work because of incomprehension of morris dancers is acceptable	

4. Glosses of "decibel (levels)" and "substantial" – eg the noise/sound/music is loud
or
it is very loud

5. Gloss of "(most players) don't even make a living from it" – eg (most players) are amateur/do not make (much) money from their music

6. *Any two glosses of:*

"(In Scotland), new pipe bands are springing up"	eg fresh groups are being formed/ flourishing/starting
"(even in London) a growing demand"	eg more interest is being shown
"organised classes for adults have started (for the first time since the 1930s)"	eg learning groups have begun/tuition is available

7. *Any two glosses of:*

"(like the idea of a) challenge"	eg (she was up for / relished a) test/trial/ attempt/difficult thing
"competent (musician)"	eg she was reasonable/ capable/proficient/adept/ adequate
"violinist and pianist and basic recorder player"	eg she plays other instruments

or
She was inspired by the Red Hot Chilli Pipers

8. They are admired/good-looking/favoured by young people/famous

9.

teamed	suggests successful combination
punching (out)	suggests impact/rhythmic quality of the music
dazzling	suggests expertise of musicians/figurative pyrotechnic quality of music/effect on audience of music
attracting new audiences	suggests growing popularity of the music

10. to lower/make more realistic/make less grand her aspirations/hopes

11.

It provides a link to the idea of difficulty / between the ideas of ease and difficulty	ie linking function, explanation
or It is an effective topic sentence introducing the idea of lack of ease	ie introductory function, explanation
or "But" introduces a contrast	

12. To acknowledge the jargon/technical nature/vagueness/inaccuracy/euphemistic nature of the expression

13. To explain/clarify what is meant by (the Gaelic expression) "Ceòl Beag".

14. Quotation of either "it grabs you" or "It'll be with you to your last day" makes inescapable or fascinating or hereditary nature of activity clear

15.

honking (effect)	suggests resemblance to a harsh/intermittent sound **or** sound produced by a klaxon or goose (bird not instrument)
or sirens	suggests wavering/ululating/harsh/deterrent quality of sound
or "horribly"	suggests cacophony/unpleasantness

16.

light years away	(effectively) suggests the distance she is from competence
enamel-stripping efforts	(effectively) suggests the abrasive/discordant nature of her efforts (accept also reference to volume)

Correct extrapolation without selective quotation may gain 1 mark.

17. *Any one idea from:*
Her efforts will be loud/discordant/annoying
or she will be playing for a long time

18. Identification of an aspect of the title relation to a feature of the passage eg

"skirl" refers to the pipes	and the passage is all about the pipes
"power" suggests potency	and the passage is all about their influence/their enduring appeal
"skirl power" is like/is a parody of "girl power"	and the writer is female

ENGLISH INTERMEDIATE 1 CRITICAL ESSAY 2012

Please see critical Essay Marking Principles on pages 69–70.

ENGLISH INTERMEDIATE 1 CLOSE READING 2013

1. She is (eg) puzzled / perplexed / confused / mystified / baffled / worried / thinking (hard)

2. (a) Gloss of "are falling out of favour" – eg they are less popular / fewer parents use them

   (b) He uses / refers to statistics/figures/the word "only"

3. Some attempt at glosses of:
   "living in a language-rich environment – and rhymes are a part of that" eg rhymes contribute to a life where language is prominent / valued / important
   "They're also tremendously valuable as a confidence-builder" eg they are useful in increasing self-esteem

4. It signals / points out / clarifies the contrast or contradiction between the claim that rhymes are not educational and the evidence which shows the opposite to be true

5. It introduces/signals an explanation or expansion of the "theory"
   or
   it introduces what the theory is

6. "nursery rhymes"
   links back (to expression used in previous paragraph)
   or
   "(the) education (of preschool children)" links back (to previous details about early learning);
   or
   "the 'music' session"
   looks forward (to details about the songs)
   or
   "(if children have) the foggiest idea (what they mean)"
   looks forward (to details about lack of understanding)

7. (a) Glosses of

"(with) actions"	eg there is movement

   and

   either

helps those who "can't sit still"	eg counters fidgeting / restlessness

   or

"help them to focus"	eg aid concentration

   (b) They don't understand them / have not thought about their meaning

   (c) (Both) very short / lacking verbs / minor sentences

8. It (neatly) shows where children's interests (now) lie
   or
   It (cleverly) introduces the change of topic (from traditional to modern)
   or
   It (clearly/appropriately) illustrates the children's short concentration span
   or
   It (clearly/appropriately) illustrates the children's flawed comprehension
   or
   It (neatly) continues the humour previously exemplified

9. Just as worms go (a long way) down into the ground | so these advertisement tunes go deeply into our consciousness

   or just as worms are invisible | so we are unaware of the presence of these tunes

   or just as (some) worms can do damage | so these tunes can harm us

   or just as worms move slowly | so these tunes go gradually into our consciousness

   or just as (some people think that) worms are repulsive | so these tunes are unattractive

10. *Any one from:*

    "suddenly"   suggests eg impetuousness

    "pipes up"   suggests eg (over-) confidence

    "firmly"   suggests eg strength of conviction

    "because the baby falls"   suggests eg logic or compassion

11. Glosses of "unsettling imagery" –
    eg ideas / pictures / concepts
    which could be violent / upsetting / disturbing

12. (a) It is being used in an unfamiliar / specialised sense / is jargon / is not being used literally

    (b) It gives an example
        of harmless violence
        or
        The violence contained in nursery rhymes
        is as harmless as that in T&J (or cartoons in general)
        or
        Idea of it using the known
        to explain the unknown

13. (a) Selection of or reference to a relevant element from the final paragraph
        relation of that to a relevant aspect elsewhere in the passage

        For example,

        "something that involves language and action (and a handover of learning)" | revisits idea of content of rhymes or idea of movement

        "They're a springboard into the world of books" / "if children know rhymes, they can open a book" | revisits idea of familiarity with rhymes helping with literacy

        "Educationally they're a wonderfully flexible tool" | revisits (the idea of) "an educational value"

        "It would be a tragedy if they disappeared" | revisits "it's sad that so many parents don't even think about nursery rhymes" **or** the title

    (b) Agreement or disagreement acceptable – mark is for any relevant point to support stated reaction

ENGLISH INTERMEDIATE 1 CRITICAL ESSAY 2009 TO 2013 EXAMS

Marking Principles for the Critical Essay are as follows:

- The essay should first be read to establish whether it achieves success in **all** the Performance Criteria for Grade C, including relevance and the standards for technical accuracy outlined in Note 1 below.
- If minimum standards are not achieved in any **one** or more of the Performance Criteria, the maximum mark which can be awarded is 11.
- If minimum standards have been achieved, then the supplementary marking grids will allow you to place the work on a scale of marks out of 25.
- The Category awarded and the mark should be placed at the end of the essay.

Notes:

1. *Mainly accurate*
   Although a few errors may be present, spelling, vocabulary and sentence structures will be sufficiently accurate to convey the candidate's meaning at first reading.

2. *Using the Category descriptions*
   - Categories are not grades. Although derived from performance criteria at C and the indicators of excellence for Grade A, the four categories are designed primarily to assist with placing each candidate response at an appropriate point on a continuum of achievement. Assumptions about final grades or association of final grades with particular categories should not be allowed to influence objective assessment.

   - Once an essay has been deemed to pass the basic criteria, it does not have to meet all the suggestions for Category II (for example) to fall into that Category. More typically there will be a spectrum of strengths and weaknesses which span categories.

GRADE C
Performance Criteria

   (*a*) *Understanding*
      As appropriate to task, the response demonstrates understanding of the main point(s) of the text(s) through some reference to relevant areas of content.

   (*b*) *Analysis*
      The response describes some of the more obvious ways in which aspects of structure/style/language contribute to meaning/effect/impact.

   (*c*) *Evaluation*
      The response contains a stated or implied personal reaction to the content or style of the text(s), supported by some textual reference.

   (*d*) *Expression*
      Language conveys meaning clearly and a generally relevant line of thought is discernible; spelling, grammar and punctuation are mainly accurate.

      It should be noted that the term "text" encompasses printed, audio or film/video text(s) which may be literary (fiction or non-fiction) or may relate to aspects of media or language.

Language Questions 9 - 10

- The "text" which should be dealt with in a language question is the research which the pupil has done. Examples taken from their research must be there for you to see.

- However, to demonstrate understanding and analysis related to these examples there has to be some ability to make comparisons or to group words of similar kinds to make a point about the use of language.

Intermediate 1 Critical Essay Supplementary Advice

This advice, which is supplementary to the published Performance Criteria, is designed to assist with the placing of scripts within the full range of marks. However, the Performance Criteria as published give the primary definitions. The mark range for each Category is identified.

IV 8–11	III 12–15	II 16–19	I 20–25
An essay which falls into this category may do so for a variety of reasons.	**Understanding** • Knowledge of the text(s), and a **basic understanding** of the main point(s) will be used	**Understanding** • Knowledge of the text(s), and an **understanding** of the main point(s) will be used	**Understanding** • Knowledge of the text(s), and an **understanding** of the main point(s) or **central concerns** will be used
	to provide a **discernibly relevant** response to the question.	to provide a response **generally relevant** to the question.	to provide a response **relevant** to the question.
It could be • that it fails to achieve the criterion of "mainly accurate"	• Some reference to the relevant **areas of content** will be made in the course of the response.	• Some reference to the **text(s) or more generally to its content** will be made in the course of the response.	• Some reference to the **text(s) as well as to its content** will be made in the course of the response.
• or that any knowledge and understanding of the material is not used to provide a discernible line of thought	**Analysis** • There will be a **description** of some obvious techniques which add to the meaning or impact of the text(s).	**Analysis** • An **attempt** will be made **to explain** how some obvious techniques add to the meaning or impact of the text(s).	**Analysis** • There will be an **explanation** of how some obvious techniques add to the meaning or impact of the text(s).
• or that personal reaction/opinion is unconvincing • or that discussion of techniques is not sufficiently related to the point being made	**Evaluation** • There will be some engagement with the text(s) and a **personal reaction** to it will be stated or implied.	**Evaluation** • There will be some engagement with the text(s) and a **personal opinion** will be stated or implied.	**Evaluation** • There will be some engagement with the text(s) and a **basic evaluation** will be stated or implied.
• or that the answer is simply too thin.	**Expression** • Language will convey meaning clearly. Spelling, grammar and punctuation are mainly accurate.	**Expression** • Language will convey meaning clearly. Spelling, grammar and punctuation are mainly accurate.	**Expression** • Language will convey meaning clearly. Spelling, grammar and punctuation are mainly accurate.